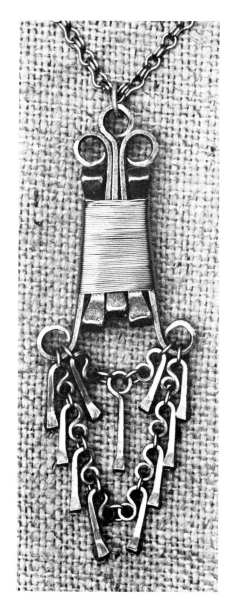

Horseshoe-Nail Crafting

By Hans Carlbom

**LiTTLE
CRAFT BOOK
SERIES**

STERLING
PUBLISHING CO., INC. NEW YORK

Oak Tree Press Co., Ltd.
London & Sydney

SAUNDERS OF TORONTO, Ltd., Don Mills, Canada

Little Craft Book Series

Aluminum and Copper Tooling
Appliqué and Reverse Appliqué
Balsa Wood Modelling
Bargello Stitchery
Beads Plus Macramé
Big-Knot Macramé
Candle-Making
Cellophane Creations
Ceramics by Slab
Coloring Papers
Corn-Husk Crafts
Corrugated Carton Crafting
Cosmetics You Can Make
Crafting with Nature's Materials
Creating Silver Jewelry with Beads
Creating with Beads
Creating with Burlap
Creating with Flexible Foam
Creative Lace-Making with Thread and Yarn
Cross Stichery
Curling, Coiling and Quilling

Enamel without Heat
Felt Crafting
Finger Weaving: Indian Braiding
Flower Pressing
Folding Table Napkins
Greeting Cards You Can Make
Hooked and Knotted Rugs
Horseshoe-Nail Crafting
How to Add Designer Touches to Your Wardrobe
Ideas for Collage
Junk Sculpture
Lacquer and Crackle
Leathercrafting
Macramé
Make Your Own Elegant Jewelry
Make Your Own Rings and Other Things
Making Paper Flowers
Making Picture Frames
Making Shell Flowers
Masks
Metal and Wire Sculpture
Model Boat Building

Monster Masks
Mosaics with Natural Stones
Nail Sculpture
Needlepoint Simplified
Off-Loom Weaving
Organic Jewelry You Can Make
Patchwork and Other Quilting
Potato Printing
Puppet-Making
Repoussage
Scissorscraft
Scrimshaw
Sculpturing with Wax
Sewing without a Pattern
Starting with Stained Glass
Stone Grinding and Polishing
String Things You Can Create
Tissue Paper Creations
Tole Painting
Trapunto: Decorative Quilting
Whittling and Wood Carving

Translated by Kenneth T. Dutfield   *Adapted by Eric W. Smith*

Front cover color photograph by Martin Jacobs

All other photographs by Mustadfors Bruks AB, C. A. Carlson and J. O. Swensson

This book was originally published by ICA-Förlaget AB under the title "Hobbyarbeten med hästskosöm"

© 1973, 1972 by Hans Carlbom and ICA-Förlaget AB, Västerås, Sweden

Published by Sterling Publishing Co, Inc.
419 Park Avenue South, New York 10016
Distributed in Canada by Saunders of Toronto, Ltd., Don Mills, Ontario
British edition published by Oak Tree Press Co., Ltd., Nassau, Bahamas
Distributed in Australia and New Zealand by Oak Tree Press Co., Ltd.,
P.O. Box J34, Brickfield Hill, Sydney 2000, N.S.W.
Distributed in the United Kingdom and elsewhere in the British Commonwealth
by Ward Lock Ltd., 116 Baker Street, London W 1
Manufactured in the United States of America   *All rights reserved*
Library of Congress Catalog Card No.: 73-83450
Sterling ISBN 0–8069–5280–6 Trade   Oak Tree 7061–2463–4
5281–4 Library

Contents

Before You Begin

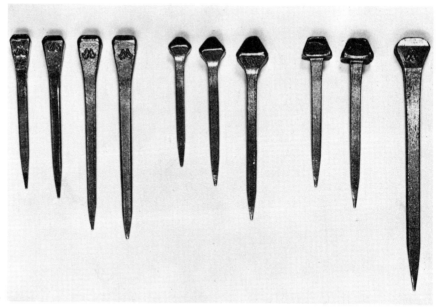

Illus. 1.

New applications are constantly being found for old, well known objects. Horseshoe nails have been in use for many, many years, but their suitability for crafting was not discovered until very recently. In fact, this is probably the first book on the subject.

Horseshoe nails are extremely versatile, and you can make a wide range of interesting objects by simply bending and soldering them. Pendants, rings, various decorations, candlesticks, mirror frames, and horseshoe-nail "paintings" are a few of the objects covered in this book. But there are dozens of additional possibilities. And all you need for horseshoe-nail crafting are a few simple tools and a supply of nails—hardly any expense at all.

There are four different types of nails, all suitable for horseshoe-nail crafting. However, one type usually looks better in a given design than another, so don't use them at random. The four types (shown in Illus. 1) are, from left to right: *J* numbers 4, 6, 8, and 10; *T* numbers 3, 5, and 8; *TIH* numbers 4 and 7; and *REG* number 12. Most of the designs in this book are made from *J* number 8 nails. A list of supply houses is in the back of the book.

4

Illus. 2. After you become familiar with the basic techniques of horseshoe-nail crafting, try making this interesting hanging decoration.

5

Bending the Horseshoe Nail

Horseshoe nails are made from soft iron, and you should have no trouble at all bending them. Try it with just a pair of pliers and your hands. If you do encounter difficulties, grip the head of the nail in a second pair of pliers. You will seldom need a hammer.

Bending horseshoe nails to make any of the designs described in this book requires very few tools—a pair of pliers with an adjustable grip, a vice, and several sections of steel pipe of assorted sizes (Illus. 3). Firmly clamp the section of steel pipe (of whatever size your design requires) in the vice. You can clamp it either horizontally or vertically, depending on which way you find more convenient.

Lay the point of the nail on the steel pipe and

Illus. 3. Bend horseshoe nails over steel pipes. You will need several pipes, of assorted sizes.

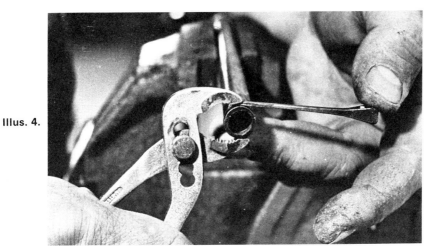

Illus. 4.

grip it with pliers (Illus. 4). Bend the nail down with your thumb (Illus. 5) until it comes in contact with the bottom jaw of the pliers (Illus. 6). Move the nail up, grip it again with the pliers (Illus. 7), and bend it down (Illus. 8). Make sure that the curved part of the nail is flush against the steel pipe. Otherwise the finished shape will be more oval than round.

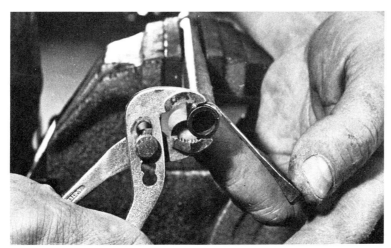

Illus. 5.

7

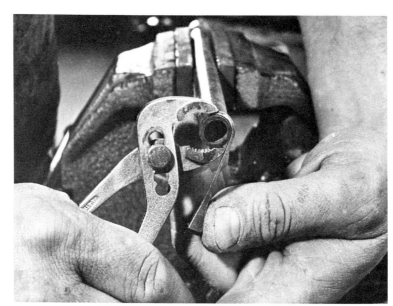

Illus. 6

Illus. 7.

8

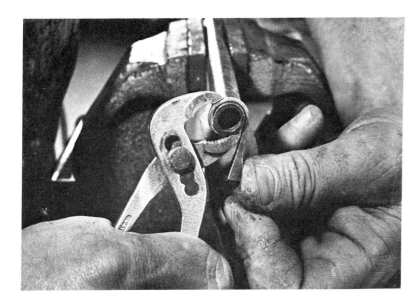

You can also bend horseshoe nails into square shapes. Hold the pointed end of the nail in the pliers (at a right angle to the pliers) and bend it down. This forms the first side of the square. To make the second side, grip the nail at a point equal to the first length, and bend the nail down again. Do the same for the third side. It's a good idea, before you start bending, to measure the nail, just to make sure that you're not making the sides too big. Otherwise you might not be able to form a square. (See Illus. 9 for two examples of square shapes.)

Illus. 9. Here are two basic square shapes. You can make your square shapes larger or smaller, or bend them at different angles, to suit your design.

Experiment with a few nails, just to get an idea of the shapes you can form. There are many possibilities—you can form all sorts of curves, triangles, and uneven shapes, as well as variations on the basic circle and square. Illus. 10 shows a few suggestions.

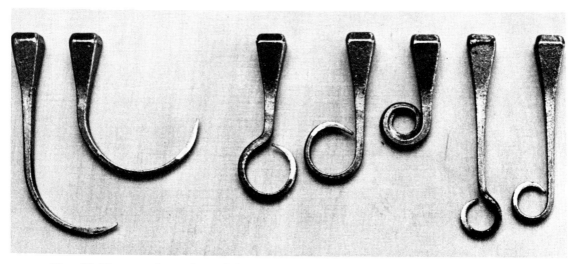

Illus. 10. These are just a few of the many shapes you can make with horseshoe nails.

10

Joining without Soldering

Although most of the projects in this book involve soldering, you can make many horseshoe-nail creations with nothing more than the nails and some iron wire.

Hooking-Up

Simply hooking nails together can lead to the creation of many bracelets, chains, necklaces, and pendants. Try making the unique necklace shown in Illus. 11. The technique is remarkably easy. Bend the pointed end of the nail into a small circle, but don't close it up. Then bend the nail at its mid-point. Leave a small space, about the width of a nail, between the head of the nail and the small circle. Repeat this process for every nail required by your design. (There are 70 in the necklace in Illus. 11, but this number is arbitrary, and you can increase or decrease this amount.)

After you have bent all the nails, begin joining them. Hook similar sections together. In other words, hook each circle to the circle of the next nail, and each mid-point to the mid-point of the nail following it. Then, with the pliers, press the head and circle of each nail together so that the circle and the space between the head of the nail and the circle are closed up. *Note:* Some types of horseshoe nails have small trademarks on their heads. Your design will look more attractive if the trademarks of all the nails face in the same direction.

Wire Binding

Wire binding is another method by which you can avoid soldering. The only material you need, besides nails and steel pipe, is a quantity of both a thin and a thick iron wire (Illus. 12).

Make an interesting, solid, decorative pendant to get the feel of the technique. The first step is to form the ends of five large (*REG #*12) nails into small circles. Bend one of the five into the shape of the center nail in Illus. 13. Lay the five side by side, in the configuration shown in the picture of the finished pendant (Illus. 13). The trademarks should all be facing away from the center nail. Now, hold the nails firmly together and wrap the thin iron wire round them as tightly as you can. Cut the wire with wire-cutting nippers. The wire and position of the nails will lock the pendant together.

Next, bend ten smaller nails into the shape shown in the picture of the finished pendant. Form the end of one additional nail into a slightly larger circle, then bend it into a shape identical to that of the large center nail above it. Now, using the thicker, less pliable iron wire, form and cut (with the wire-cutting nippers) a quantity of small rings. The best way to do this is to wrap 2 or 3 feet (60 or 90 cm.) of the wire round a small steel pipe and cut off the rings from the resultant coil as you need them.

Finally, hook all the nails together with rings, following Illus. 13, and hang them from the two outside larger nails. Attach a ring to the large

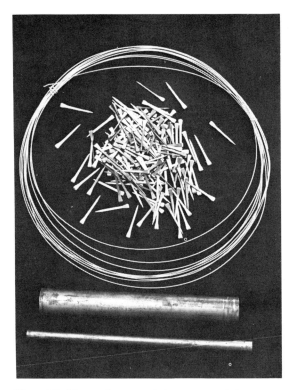

Illus. 12. The only materials you need for wire binding are horseshoe nails, iron wire, and steel pipe.

center nail, run a small chain through it, and your pendant is ready for display.

These basic methods have endless possibilities. Experiment with them—there are many beautiful designs that you can make without using any solder at all.

Finishing Your Design

All nails eventually begin to rust if exposed to moisture or the elements. Therefore, if there is even a remote chance that your horseshoe-nail design might come in contact with dampness, you should varnish it after you make it.

Clean all dirt and grease from the finished design and dry it completely. Then apply a coat of clear, colorless lacquer over the entire surface. You can use a liquid lacquer, but an aerosol spray covers hard-to-reach areas better. (*Caution:* If you varnish designs that have been soldered, make sure that the solder is cold and the iron in another room. Lacquer is extremely flammable.)

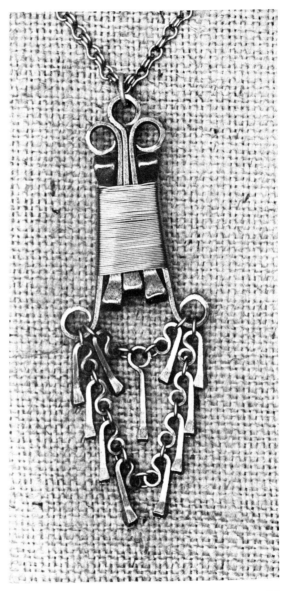

Illus. 13. You can make many decorations and pieces of jewelry without soldering.

Soldering Horseshoe Nails

Soldering opens up whole new vistas for the horseshoe-nail crafter. By soldering, you can make a limitless variety of designs of all sizes and shapes. And soldered constructions will, under normal circumstances, last forever.

For soldering you need a pointed, electric soldering iron that reaches a heat of at least 600° to 700° F. (316° to 371° C.) If you have access to a propane torch, it is a little easier to work with, but also less safe. You will also need some fireproof asbestos tiles or flat bricks, flux, and solder. It is best to use a solder that has a small quantity of silver in it. The silver increases the strength of the solder.

For your first soldering project, try making a few simple clothes hooks (Illus. 14). Bend the

Illus. 14. Just for a change, try hanging your clothes on these sturdy hooks.

14

Place a small quantity of flux on the surfaces you intend to join. Now heat the area to be soldered until you reach the melting point of the solder. When this point is reached, apply the solder (Illus. 15). Hold the end of the solder against the tip of the soldering iron and let the molten solder flow into and over the joint. For some designs, you may have to hold the soldering iron just above the joint and let the melted solder drop into it to avoid accidentally jarring a nail out of place.

As soon as the solder has flowed into and covered the joint, remove the soldering iron and go on to the next piece.

Remember not to use more solder than necessary. A big lump of solder doesn't increase the strength of the joint at all, and looks ugly. A soldered joint should be as nearly invisible as you can make it. (CAUTION: Be very careful with the flux. It contains poisonous and corrosive acid. If you get any on your fingers, wash it off immediately in warm water.)

After the solder has cooled and hardened, remove any flux left on the nails. Rinse the clothes hooks in hot water and scrub gently with a brush, then dry thoroughly. Smooth down any lumps of solder with steel wool or a thin steel-wire brush. Clean the nails and, if you wish, varnish as described on page 13. To hang the clothes hook, just place it against the wall and hammer either a horseshoe or ordinary nail through the triangular space formed by the junction of the heads of the three nails.

nails into the shapes shown in Illus. 14 and blunt the tip of the nail on which the clothing will hang by turning it down with the pliers. Clean any dirt or grease from the surfaces to be soldered (the heads of all three nails) and then arrange the nails in their proper positions. Make sure that there is no gap between the surfaces you are soldering together.

Horseshoe-Nail Jewelry

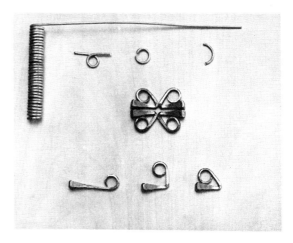

Jewelry made from horseshoe nails has a uniqueness and beauty all its own. Interesting patterns and pleasing weight and texture make them desirable ornaments for anyone, no matter what age or sex.

A Pendant and Bracelet Set

Aside from the horseshoe nails, all you need for the pendant and bracelet set in Illus. 16 is thick iron wire. Form the pointed ends of the

Illus. 17. Bend the nails and solder them into units of four nails, as shown.

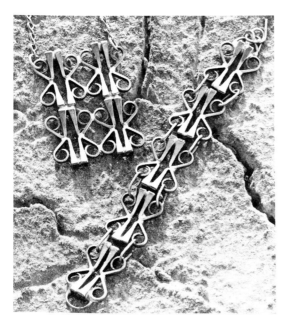

Illus. 16. A matching pendant and bracelet set is a unique adornment.

nails into small circles, bend them over in the middle, and arrange them in groups of four nails, as shown in Illus. 17. You can make the gap in the middle wider (as in the pendant) or narrower if you wish. Solder the four nails together. To make the pendant, just solder four of these units together, attach iron rings to the outside, upper circles, and hook the ends of a chain to the rings. To make the bracelet, hook four or five units together with iron rings (made from two, instead of one, loops of the coil you formed earlier), and solder a semi-circular piece of iron wire to each end of the bracelet.

Attach one or two rings to one end of the bracelet. Then make another ring, this time with lengthened ends (shown between the ring and the coil in Illus. 17), and hook it onto the ring or rings you just attached.

A Horseshoe-Nail Ring

You can construct a variety of interesting rings from small horseshoe nails (J 4) and sheet metal. Cut or saw a piece of sheet metal to the shape shown in Illus. 18. Smooth off the edges of the metal with a file or grindstone and solder on the shaped nails. Then, and not before, bend the metal strip over a piece of steel pipe or a wooden dowel. Make sure that the piece of pipe or dowel is approximately the size of your finger. (Illus. 20 shows two additional ring designs.)

Illus. 18. Form the nails and cut the sheet metal, solder the nails to the metal, and bend the metal to fit your finger.

17

Illus. 19. Glass beads are available in various sizes and shapes in craft and hobby shops.

Pendants

There are no restrictions of design or shape that you need observe when making horseshoe-nail pendants. Look through the designs on the next few pages (Illus. 20, 21, 22, 23, 24, and 25). As you can see, each pendant is very different from all of the others. Make a few of them, and get a feel for the techniques—but don't stop there. Experiment with the nails and see what *you* can come up with. Sketch possible designs on a sheet of paper and, if you hit upon a particularly

attractive one, make it! You will know how if you learn the techniques.

The pendants in the illustrations mentioned earlier require only nails, solder, thick iron wire, and glass beads. The glass beads are available in several colors and shapes in craft and hobby shops (Illus. 19). Use a two-part glue for glueing the glass to the metal—either a synthetic resin glue or an epoxy adhesive, both of which are sold in craft shops and hardware stores. To make the designs, just follow the pictures.

Illus. 20.

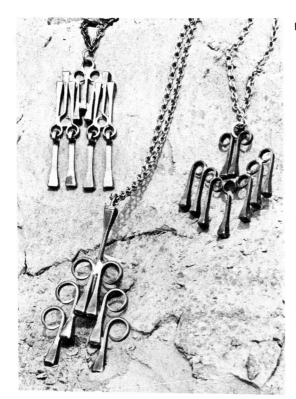

Illus. 22.

Illus. 23.

Illus. 25. The pendant design at the bottom of the photograph was made from "frost nails," which are no longer manufactured. However, you can substitute other nails.

A Belt Buckle

If you're tired of dull, unexciting belt buckles, try making one from horseshoe nails. Use small horseshoe nails, and construct the buckle by following the picture (Illus. 26). Make the cross-bar and the catch from thick, stiff iron wire.

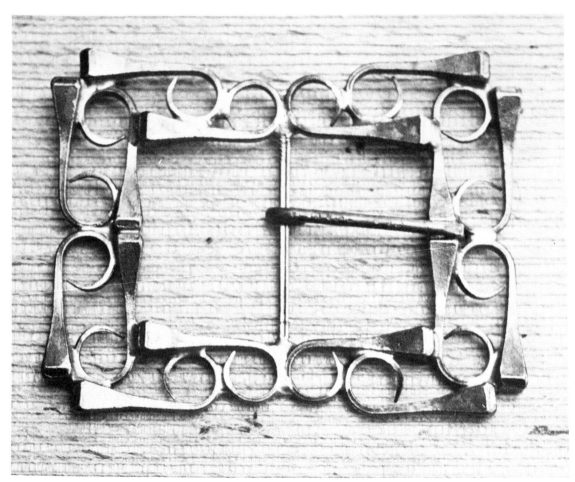

Illus. 26. Any belt will look better with this horseshoe-nail belt buckle.

Hanging Decorations

Illus. 27.

Illus. 28.

Hanging decorations make any room more attractive. Illus. 27 through 33 show some possibilities. Solder very carefully when making hanging decorations—their delicate appearance is ruined by large lumps of solder.

25

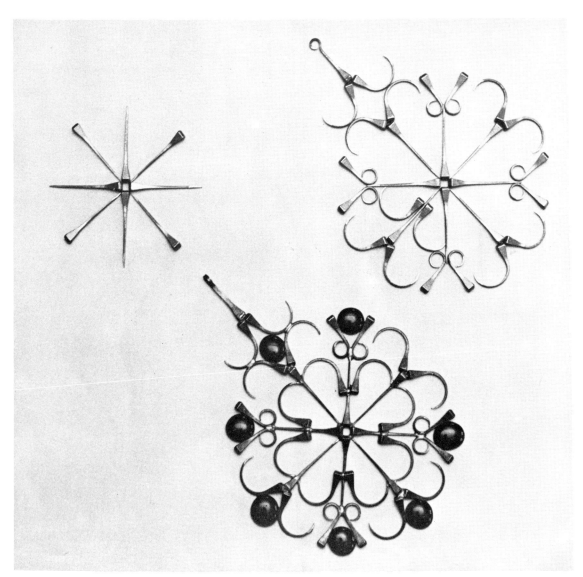

Illus. 29. Construct hanging decorations such as this by building from the middle outwards.

Illus. 30.

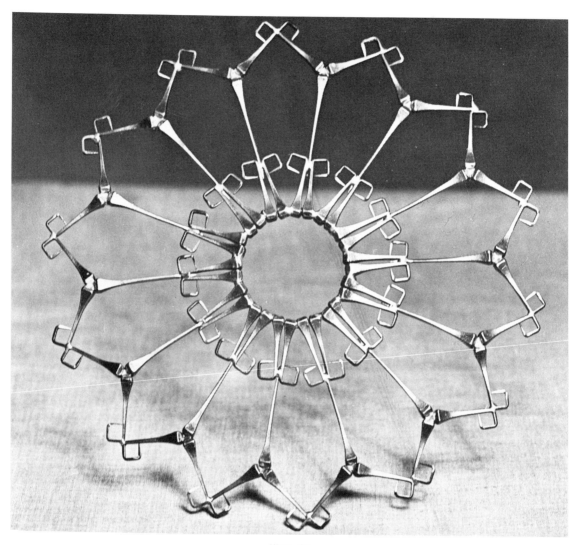

Illus. 31.

Illus. 32.

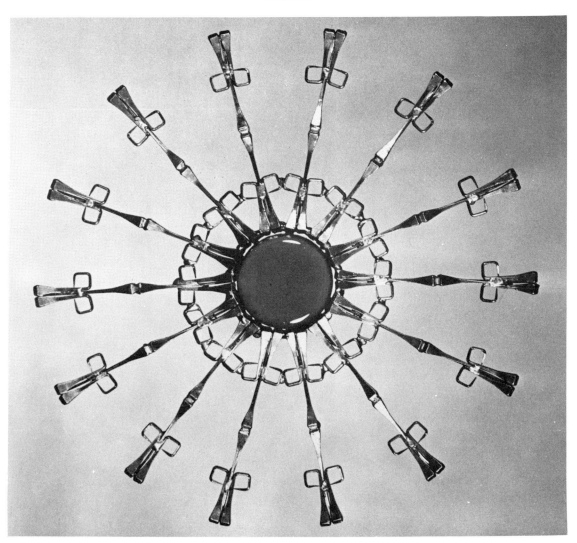

Illus. 33. Form the
bell shape in a
cylindrical piece of
wood.

Illus. 33 shows the procedure for making a bell-shaped hanging decoration. Bend 16 nails over a large steel pipe and then make eight S-shapes from them.

Use a cylindrical piece of wood with a conical hole in one end to hold the nails while you solder them. The wood should have roughly the same diameter as the bell shape you are making.

If you can't find a suitable piece of wood, you can try a tin can. Find one with the right diameter, then tape the S-shapes to the can so that the points all meet in the middle of the can. However, soldering is much trickier with this arrangement, so it's better to use a piece of wood if you possibly can. (Illus. 34 shows the finished decoration.)

Illus. 34. The bell shape
will be balanced only
if the space between
each S-shape is equal.

Functional Horseshoe-Nail Decorations

Your horseshoe-nail creations can have practical, as well as ornamental, uses. You can use them as holders or bases for a variety of objects. The horseshoe nails contrast very nicely with a simple, glowing candle, an old tea or coffee pot, or a gleaming mirror.

Candlesticks

To make the candlesticks shown on the next few pages you will need, besides nails and glass beads, several widths of steel pipe and some sheet metal. The steel pipe serves as a candle-holder. Just cut a short section, of a suitable size, with a hack-saw, and solder, following the procedure detailed earlier (page 15). Sheet metal is used in several of the designs as a base for the section of steel pipe.

Try making a hanging candlestick first (Illus. 35). Use the techniques discussed on page 30 to make the lower part of the candlestick. Use sheet metal for a base for the candle-holder. Hook the lower part to the upper part, and then just add a candle.

There are many types of standing candlesticks. Illus. 36 and 37 show the procedure for constructing one kind. Solder 4 large (*REG #12*) nails to the candle-holder as shown (left). Bend the heads at right angles (90°). Solder a nail to each of the legs formed by the large nails (see Illus. 37). Then solder on the remaining parts. The finished candlestick is shown in Illus. 38. This candlestick can also serve as a coffee- or tea-pot warmer (Illus. 39).

Illus. 35.

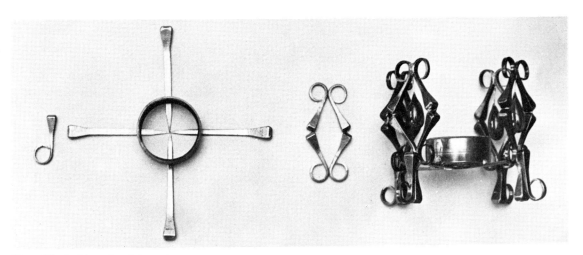

Illus. 36. Solder the 4 legs together and add the supporting legs, then solder 4 units of 4 nails (shown in the center) each together and attach them.

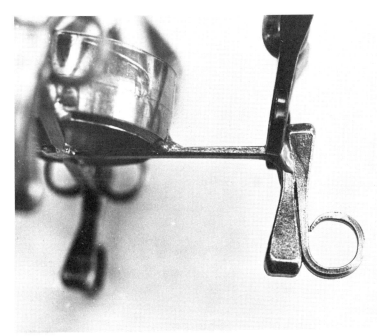

Illus. 37. Attach a supporting leg to the head of each large (REG #12) nail.

Illus. 38. The large double candlestick shown here was made from "frost nails," which are no longer manufactured. Other nails (REG #12, for instance) can be substituted.

Illus. 39. The candle-
stick shown in
Illus. 37 can double as
a coffee- or tea-pot
warmer. If you turn
the hanging decor-
ation shown in
Illus. 33 over, you can
use it as a candlestick.

Sconces

Illus. 40 and 41 show two types of horseshoe-nail sconces. You may need to use a clamp when soldering on the candle-holder for the sconce in Illus. 41.

Illus. 40. Your candles will glow to greater effect in these horse-shoe-nail sconces.

Illus. 41.

A Chandelier

The large, delicate chandelier in Illus. 42 is surprisingly easy to construct. Make 15 S-shapes (each from two nails) and start soldering. Form the top and bottom sections of the body of the chandelier in a round piece of wood, following the procedure on page 30. Make sure that the five candle-holders, and the nails supporting them, are evenly spaced. Otherwise the chandelier will be off-balance.

NOTE: For large constructions such as this, or for anything that will be subjected to heat above 300°F. (149°C.), you may need to *braze* the nails, rather than solder them. Brazing makes much stronger joints than soldering, and therefore is sometimes necessary when the joints must carry a large amount of weight or stand up against greater than usual stresses. Use a solder containing a large proportion of silver. This kind of solder must be heated to temperatures around 1300°F. (704°C.) with a propane torch. This great heat gives the nail a blue color however, and quite a lot of finishing is required. Because of the danger involved, only adults, who know what they're doing, should try brazing.

Mirror Frames

A horseshoe-nail design forms an interesting border for a mirror.

The first step is, of course, to find a mirror. Be sure to use one with ground edges. The whole rim of the mirror will be visible, and if you decorate one without ground edges, it will detract from the total effect.

Lay the mirror on the asbestos tiles on which you do your soldering. Insert straight nails under the mirror (see Illus. 43 for placement) about $\frac{5}{8}$ inch (16 millimetres). These serve as fastenings. Check carefully to make sure that all the nails are equidistant from each other (that is, distance along the rim, *not* across the mirror) and that each

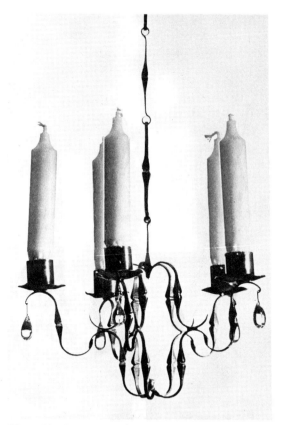

Illus. 42. Construction of a chandelier requires attention to details, but the result is well worth it.

Illus. 43.

is exactly perpendicular to the edge of the mirror. Now begin putting the rest of the nails in place, following Illus. 43. (See Illus. 44 for a close-up.) When all the nails are properly positioned, lift out the mirror. Take great care that you don't accidentally knock any of the nails out of position.

Next, solder all the nails together. After the solder has hardened, lay the mirror in the frame. Turn the mirror and the frame over and, with the two-part glue, glue the nails to the back of the mirror (that is, the nails previously inserted under the mirror).

Cover the back with a sheet of cardboard slightly smaller than the mirror.

Illus. 45 and 46 show two additional mirror designs.

Illus. 44.

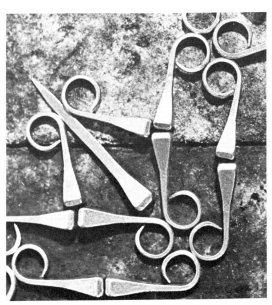

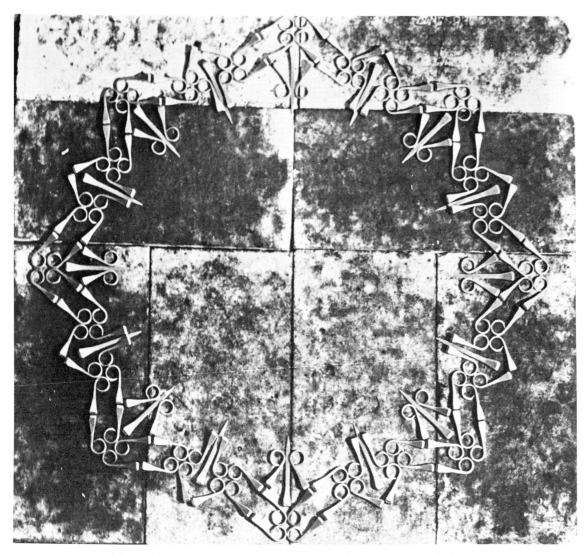

Illus. 45. This picture shows another possible mirror frame design.

Illus. 46.

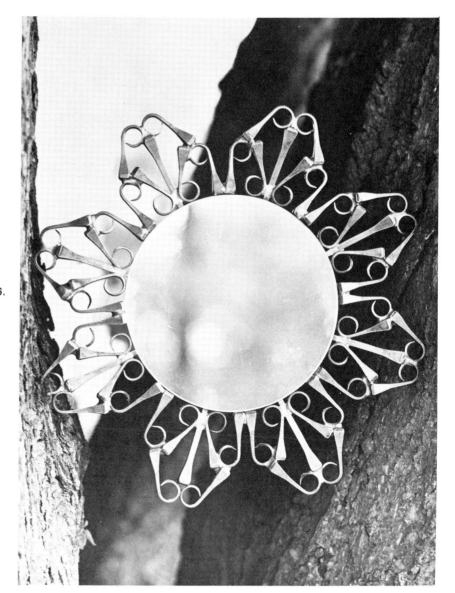

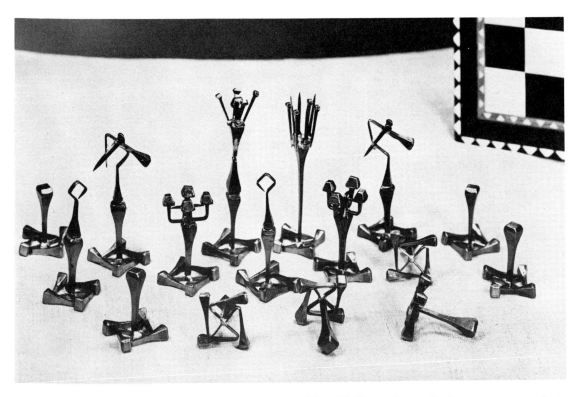

Chessmen

Next time you play chess, why not play it with a really unique set of chessmen? The pieces in Illus. 47 are: a pawn (first from left); a bishop (second from left); a knight (third from left); a rook (fifth from left); and a king (left) and queen (the two large pieces in back). When constructing the pieces, just follow the illustration.

Illus. 47. Horseshoe-nail chessmen are simple to make. All the bases are made from four nails bent at a 45° angle. Some of the pieces require you to break the pointed ends off the nails. Do this with a hack-saw.

Horseshoe-Nail "Paintings"

As you no doubt have already discovered, you can use horseshoe nails to make a large variety of jewelry, decorations, candlesticks, and other useful objects. However, you can also use these versatile nails to make both realistic and abstract "paintings." Illus. 48, 49, and 50 show a few examples. Attach your horseshoe-nail paintings (with nails or glue) to walls, pieces of wood, or fabric.

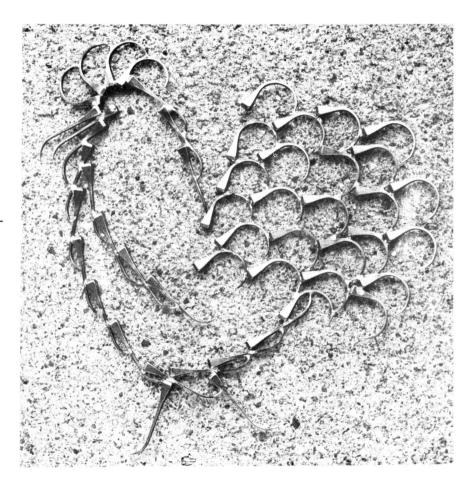

Illus. 48. Horseshoe-nail "paintings" look attractive on either outside or inside walls.

Illus. 49. The middle of the flower is made from J number 4 nails. Lay the nails on top of the J number 8 nails and bend them upwards after soldering.

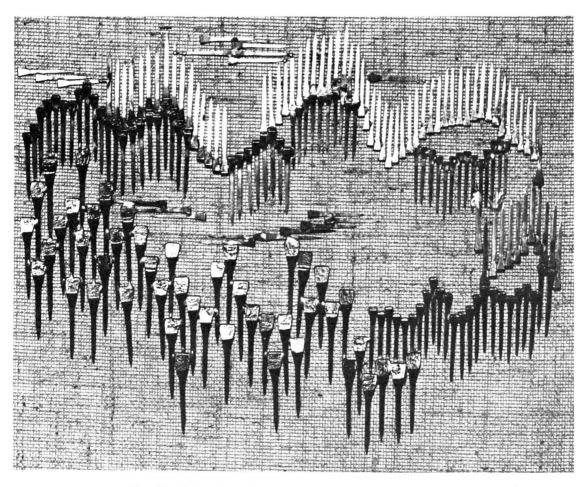

Illus. 50. Make a large "painting" such as this in several parts.

Creating Your Own Designs

Creating your own designs is not very difficult. There are a few important things you should remember, though. Don't make your design too complicated, for this may give the viewer the feeling that it is cluttered or fussy. Don't mix too many different shapes in the same design—it's better to just repeat one or two curves or patterns. If you are thinking of making a large design, construct it in sections rather than all at once. This makes it easier to visualize and construct accurately.

When you make up any horseshoe-nail design you must deal with certain practical considerations. Make sure that your creation is balanced, and that it won't tilt or tip over. And always remember to distribute the soldering points so that when the design is complete it will stick together. It's easier to make a few revisions in your design than it is to correct it after it has been soldered together.

You can get many good ideas for horseshoe-nail designs from geometric patterns, abstract or even representational paintings and sculpture, flowers, butterflies, and animals—in short, just by looking around you. Above all, use your imagination. Just sit back and relax and see what you can come up with.

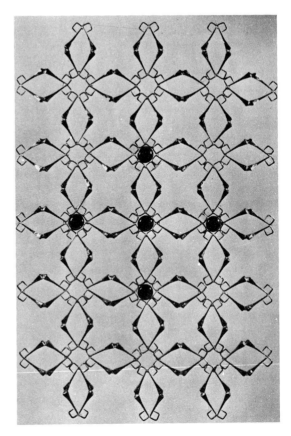

Illus. 51. Try making your own horseshoe-nail designs. Constructions such as this are fairly easy to put together and have a geometric beauty all their own. Notice also the well-distributed soldering points.

Suppliers

The horseshoe nails used for the projects in this book are manufactured by Mustadfors Bruks AB, in Sweden. They are available from the following firms:

The Birt Saddlery Co. Ltd.
468–474 Main Street, Area Code 204
Winnipeg, Manitoba
Canada

Buckerfield's Limited
P.O. Box 7000
Vancouver, B.C.
Canada

Griffith Saddlery & Leather Ltd.
P.O. Box 633
240 Norfolk Street, Area Code 519
Stratford, Ontario
Canada

Lyttel and Westaway, Pty, Ltd.
181 Clarence Street
Sydney 2000 NSW
Australia

H. W. Mangelsen and Sons, Inc.
8200 J Street
Omaha, Nebraska 68127
(Exclusive U.S. distributor for the crafts trade.)

Mustadfors Bruks AB
P.O. Box 10
S-660 10 DALS LÅNGED
Sweden

Mustad Manufacturing Co.
Old Mill Road
Porteshead near Bristol
England

Frank J. Newman Co.
Exchange Building
28 St. Georges Street
Capetown
South Africa

Index